*The Thought of the Heart*

*Eranos Lectures 2*

# THE THOUGHT OF THE HEART

*James Hillman*

Spring Publications, Inc.
Dallas, Texas

Copyright 1981 by the Eranos Foundation, Ascona, Switzerland

Printed in the United States of America by BookCrafters, Inc., Chelsea, Michigan, for Spring Publications, Inc., P.O. Box 222069, Dallas, Texas 75222

Cover design and production by Patricia Mora and Maribeth Lipscomb

*International Distributors*
Spring, Postfach, 8800 Thalwil, Switzerland
Japan Spring Sha, Inc.; 1-2-4, Nishisakaidani-Cho; Ohharano, Nishikyo-Ku; Kyoto, 610-11, Japan
Element Books Ltd; The Old Brewery Tisbury Salisbury; Wiltshire SP3 6NH; England

Library of Congress Cataloging in Publication Data

Hillman, James.
   The thought of the heart.

   (Eranos lectures ; 2)
   "A lecture presented originally at the 1979 Eranos Conference in Ascona, Switzerland, and appeared in the Eranos yearbook 48-1973"—T.p. verso.
   Includes bibliographical references.
   1. Love—Psychological aspects—Addresses, essays, lectures. 2. Psychoanalysis—Addresses, essays, lectures. 3. Jung, C. G. (Carl Gustav), 1875-1961 — Addresses, essays, lectures. I. Title. II. Series: Eranos lectures ; 2.

BF575.L8H55    1984    150.19'5    84-5462
ISBN 0-88214-402-2

Eranos Lectures series: ISSN 0743-586X

---

*Acknowledgments*

"The Thought of the Heart" was a lecture presented originally at the 1979 Eranos Conference in Ascona, Switzerland, and appeared in the *Eranos Yearbook* 48—1973 (Frankfurt am Main: Insel Verlag, 1981), pp. 133-82. It is here published with the kind permission of the Eranos Foundation.

# CONTENTS

Part One
## THE CAPTIVE HEART  1

*Coeur de Lion*  6
*The Heart of Harvey*  11
*The Heart of Augustine*  16

Part Two
## THE HEART OF BEAUTY  24

*Kalon kagathon and Jung*  33
*"Going over to another order"*  37
*The lion roars at the enraging desert*  41
*The White Sulphur and the Illusions of the Heart*  44

*"Speech is not of the tongue, but of the heart. The tongue is merely the instrument with which one speaks. He who is dumb is dumb in his heart, not in his tongue... As you speak, so is your heart."*

Paracelsus[1]

## I. THE CAPTIVE HEART

You who have been privileged at some time during these last twenty years or thirty to have been here for a lecture by Henry Corbin have been present at a manifestation of the thought of the heart. You have been witness to its creative imagination, its theophanic power of bringing the divine face into visibility. You will also know in your hearts that the communication of the thought of the heart proceeds in that fashion of which he was master, as a *récit,* an account of the imaginal life as a journey among imaginal essences, an account of the essential. In him imagination was utterly presence. One was in presence of imagination itself, that imagination in which and by which the spirit moves from the heart towards all origination.

You also have already seen and heard the themes that I shall be attempting this afternoon as they were embodied in the physical intensity of that living man, Henry Corbin: the thought of the heart as sovereign and noble, as joyous, as subtle as an animal, bold, courageous and encouraging, as delighting in intellectual forms and

---

1 Paracelsus (Sudhoff-Matthiessen, ed.) Part I, 14:276–77, as quoted by J. Jacobi, *Paracelsus:* Selected Writings, London: Routledge, 1951, p. 241.

fierce in their defense, ever-extending equally in its compassion and in its visionary power, forming a beauty in the language of images.

Because of what he has done here – and is continuing to do here, since the presence of a person does not depend only on his visibility, the invisible Henry Corbin is among us – because of him, the basis of our work has already been done. We do not have to establish the primary principle: that the thought of the heart is the thought of images, that the heart is the seat of imagination, that imagination is the authentic voice of the heart, so that if we speak from the heart we must speak imaginatively. Because the primary principle has already been given by him, we may explore tributaries of the main stream.

Our job this afternoon will be less to inspire the heart by recitations of life in the imaginal as he did, and more to rediscover the heart in its immediate actual imaginings, in its exile, in an imagination which Corbin calls "captive" (*SB*: 146), where the thought of the heart has become adulterated in our contemporary heart diseases: sentimentality of personalism, brutalism of efficiency, aggrandizement of power, and simple religious effusionisms.

It was Henry Corbin's gift to enable us to experience in this room thoughts that come from another language and culture, as if they were of our own hearts. He spoke from within his speech; he was his words. This rhetorical imaginative power is *himma* of which Corbin writes in his study of Ibn 'Arabi[2]:

> This power of the heart is what is specifically designated by the word *himma*, a word whose content is perhaps best suggested by the Greek word *enthymesis*, which signifies the act of meditating, conceiving, imagining, projecting, ardently desiring – in other words, of having (something) present in the *thymos*, which is vital force, soul, heart, intention, thought, desire... (*CI*: 224).

As he goes on to explain, this *himma*, the thought of the heart in Ibn

[2] The works of Henry Corbin quoted in the text are: *Creative Imagination in the Sufism of Ibn Arabi*, Bollingen Series, Princeton Univ. Press, 1969 (French, Paris: Flammarion, 1958) = *CI.*; *Spiritual Body and Celestial Earth*, Bollingen Series, Princeton Univ. Press, 1977 (French, Paris: Buchet-Chastel, 1960) = *SB*; *The Man of Light in Iranian Sufism*, Boulder & London: Shambhala, 1978 = *ML*.

# The Thought of the Heart

'Arabi, is so powerful as to make essentially real a being external to the person who is in this condition of *enthymesis*. Himma creates as 'real' the figures of the imagination, those beings with whom we sleep and walk and talk, the angels and daimones who, as Corbin says, are outside the imagining faculty itself. Himma is that mode by which the images, which we believe we make up, are actually presented to us as not of our making, as genuinely created, as authentic creatures. And, as Corbin goes on to say, without the gift of himma we fall into the modern psychological illusions. We misunderstand the mode of being of these images, the figures in our dreams or the persons of our imaginings. We believe these figures are subjectively real when we mean imaginally real: the illusion that we made them up, own them, that they are part of us, phantasms. Or, we believe these figures are externally real when we mean essentially real – the illusions of parapsychology and hallucinations. We confuse imaginal with subjective and internal, and we mistake essential for external and objective.

We cannot go further this afternoon without this background in Corbin, because we are bereft in our culture of an adequate psychology and philosophy of the heart, and therefore also of the imagination. Our hearts cannot apprehend that they are imaginatively thinking hearts, because we have so long been told that the mind thinks and the heart feels, and that imagination leads us astray from both. Even when the heart is allowed its reasons, they are those of faith or of feeling, for we have forgotten that philosophy itself – the most complex and profound demonstration of thought – is not 'wisdom' or 'truth' in an abstract sense of 'sophic'.[3] Rather, philosophy begins in a philos arising in the heart of our blood, together with the lion, the wound, and the rose. If we would recover the imaginal we must first recover its organ, the heart, and its kind of philosophy.

Philosophy enunciates the world in the images of words. It must arise in the heart in order to mediate the world truly, since, as Cor-

---

3 Cf. below p. 162 on "sophia", the other half of the word *philosophy*.

bin says, it is that subtle organ which perceives the correspondences between the subtleties of consciousness and the levels of being. This intelligence takes place by means of images which is a third possibility between mind and world. Each image coordinates within itself qualities of consciousness and qualities of world, speaking in one and the same image of the interpenetration of consciousness and world, but always and only as image which is primary to what it coordinates. This imaginational intelligence resides in the heart: "intelligence of the heart" connotes a simultaneous knowing and loving by means of imagining.

If such philosophy is an event of the heart, events of the heart may be conceived as philosophic. The heart's work is imaginational thought, even if disguised in philosophies that seem without images and without heart. This imaginational thought can even be disguised in philosophies or psychologies of its own nature, that is, in theories of the heart. We shall have to turn to some of these in order to recover from those disguises a true philosophy originating in the imaginal heart itself, the heart of Corbin.

But first we must relate the imaginal heart of Corbin with the heart of depth psychology, of Freud. For Freud provides the paradigmatic occasion for the appearance of the thought of the heart within that Western modern consciousness which is bereft of a philosophy for adequately meditating its own heart. Though the relation of Freud to Corbin may seem strained, it is worth every effort, for Corbin can save Freud from the Fall, from reduction downward. The relation allows us to look at Freud always with the imaginal eye of Corbin.

For instance: the beginnings of psychoanalysis are marked by two signal events. Looking at them with the eye of Corbin we can see them as having the same source. These events, you will remember, are the fact that the very first patient whom Freud's colleague Josef Breuer treated by the new method fell so in love with the good old doctor, that it – this transference as it came to be called – drove Breuer out of psychoanalysis for ever.

The second event was that as the patients unburdened their hearts

# The Thought of the Heart

in detailed memory images, their stories moved from fact to fiction, from mundane recollections to fantastic inventions (*in-venio* = incursions, comings in), from history to imagination.

Love and imagination entered psychoanalysis at the same moment. From its inception psychoanalysis raised the *thymos* of the heart – which it called wishing, *Wunsch* – to priority as an explanatory principle. The patient was a creature of *enthymesis* in whom the himma was awakening. And the presence of the analyst, Freud or Breuer, became the first carrier of the imaginal figures. Transference, yes; but from where transferred? Not childhood and the downward reduction only, but Platonic childhood, and the a priori remembrance of imaginal presences transferred with us into this life and the source of its love.

When we fall in love, we begin to imagine; and when we begin to imagine, we fall in love. To this day, depth psychology is caught by the necessary connection of love and imagination which it has not yet had the philosophy to place. It has not yet read Corbin as a classic of psychoanalysis. It has stumbled into the heart without a philosophy of its thought.

Now to the disguises. When in our exile we stand in the contemporary heart and imagine from it, our images move in several directions, each one a philosophy about the heart. Let us review these commonplace imaginings as expressions of the heart in our culture.

First: my heart is my humanity, my courage to live, my strength and fierce passion. By means of it nothing is foreign to me[4]; all can be admitted to its kingdom of dignity. My most noble virtues emanate from the heart: loyalty, heroic boldness, compassion. Let us call this the heart of the Lion, Cœur de Lion.

---

4 I have subjoined to the heart of the lion the heart as locus of the *sensus communis*, the place of natural law connecting all individuals with each other and with the order of the world. How *sensus communis* perceives this order is discussed below in Part II. The various implications of the *sensus communis*, although important to heart theory, cannot find enough place in this paper. Cf. H.-G. Gadamer, *Truth and Method*, N.Y.: Seabury, 1975, pp. 19–39.

Second: my heart is an organ of the body. It is a muscle or a pump, an intricate mechanism and secret holder of my death. Let us refer to this pumping heart as the heart of Harvey.

Third: my heart is my love, my feelings, the locus of my soul and sense of person. It is the place of intimate interiority, where sin and shame and desire, and the unfathomable divine too, inhabit. Let us call this personal heart, the heart of Augustine.

### Cœur de Lion

The first of these hearts comes from folklore, astrology, symbolic medicine, physiognomy. The heart of the lion is like the sun: round and full and whole. The classical symbolisms of this heart are gold, king, redness, *sol*, sulphur, heat. It glows in the center of our being and radiates outward, magnanimous, paternal, encouraging.

Ficino said that the nature of the heart is warm and dry, and that warmth has best conformity with the universe. The thought of the lion warms so to life, is so in conformity with the world, that its thought is one with will, displaying itself in the world, enthroned as king, yellow as daylight, loud as a roar, fixed as dogma. Thought presents itself as volition, as mood, or as love, vitality, power, or imagination, and does not recognize itself as thought because it is not reflexive ratiocination, abstracted away from life, introspective.

Crucial to the heart of the lion is that it *believes,* and it believes that it does not think. So its thought appears in the world as project, desire, concern, mission. Thinking and doing together. This is the bold thought that takes us into battle, for Mars rides a red lion, and the heroes – David, Samson, Hercules – must meet the ravenous hunger for the world of deeds fulminating in his own breast.

So, the first basic characteristic of the *cœur de lion* is that its *thought does not appear as thought* because it emanates like the sun into the world and remains disguised in that conformity with its motion.

# The Thought of the Heart

A second fundamental trait of this cardiac consciousness has been described by D. H. Lawrence in his symbolic physiology:

> At the cardiac plexus... there in the center of the breast, we have a new great sun of knowledge and of being... Here I only know the delightful revelation that you are you. The wonder is no longer within me, my own dark, centrifugal exultant self. The wonder is without me. The wonder is outside me... I look with wonder, with tenderness, with joyful yearning towards that which is outside me, beyond me...[5]

The utter otherness of its direction, this movement outward and beyond, produces what Jung has called the "dark body" at the core of ego-consciousness, its blindness to itself. For, not only does this heart not know that it thinks, but its thought is completely coagulated into its objectifications. So wholly is its love and will one, itself and other one, itself and God one, that its vision of the cosmos is monistic and monarchical[6], one archai, monotheistic, and the heart always whole. Monarchical wholeheartedness characterizes its typical psychopathology, the psychopathology of *intensity*: the heart's own rhythmic systole and diastole, magnified, become intensely singled, one-sidedly either manic or depressive, roaring or lazy.

Thus, the task of consciousness for the *cœur de lion* lies in recognizing the archetypal construct of its thought, that its actions, desires and ardent beliefs are all imaginations – creations of the himma – and that what it experiences as life, love and world is its own *enthymesis* presented outside as the macrocosm.

Alchemical psychology remarkably condenses the two traits of the lion-heart – the conformity of its thought and its objectification – into the alchemical substance, sulphur[7], the principle of "com-

---

5 D. H. Lawrence, *Fantasia of the Unconscious*, London: Heinemann, Phoenix, 1961, p. 33.

6 Ph. Wolff, *Die Gekrönten*, Stuttgart: Klett, 1958, p. 182, notes that the heraldic lion always is *single*. Only one lion, like only one King.

7 Cf. *CW 14*: 134–53 for an excellent digest of alchemical passages on sulphur. Jung notes its connection with Venus (139), and Titus Burckhardt (*Alchemy*, London:

bustibility"[8], the *magna flamma*. "Where is the sulphur to be found?" asks Kramer, a 14th Century English Benedictine. "In all substances, all things in the world – metals, herbs, trees, animals, stones, are its ore."[9]

Everything that suddenly lights up, draws our joy, flares with beauty – each bush a God burning: this is the alchemical sulphur, the flammable face of the world, its phlogiston, its aureole of desire, *enthymesis* everywhere. That fat of goodness we reach toward as consumers is the active image in each thing, the active imagination of the anima mundi that fires the heart and provokes it out.

At the same time that sulphur conflagrates, it also coagulates; it is that which sticks, the mucilage, "the gum", the joiner, the stickiness of attachment.[10] Sulphur literalizes the heart's desire at the very instant that the *thymos* enthuses. Conflagration and coagulation occur together. Desire and its object become indistinguishable. What I burn with attaches me to it; I am anointed by the fat of my own desire, captive to my own enthusiasm, and thus in exile from my heart at the very moment I seem most to own it. We lose our soul in the moment of discovering it: "Sweet Helen", says Marlowe's Faustus, "make me immortal with a kiss. / Her lips suck forth my soul: see where it flies!" Hence Heraclitus had to oppose *thymos* and *psyche*: "Whatever *thymos* wishes, it buys at the expense of soul" (D.-K. 85).

<small>Stuart & Watkins, 1967, p. 140) notes its connection with *anima* or cosmic vitality of the universe experienced as the heat of the heart. In sulphur's "compulsion" and "lack of freedom" (Jung, 151–52) resides, I suggest, the problem of the captive imagination (in Corbin's sense), necessitating those operations on the heart (whitening the sulphur) which are discussed below in Part II.

8 John Read, *Through Alchemy to Chemistry*, London: Bell, 1957, p. 18.
9 "New Chemical Light" in *Hermetic Museum*, London: Stuart and Watkins, 1953, II:154.
10 Cf. Paracelsus, *The Hermetic and Alchemical Writings*, A. E. Waite, tr., N.Y.: University Books, 1967, I: 127. For some of these other attributes of sulphur – "fatness of the earth", its "very strong action", "fiery nature", "gum", and "entirely smoky", see *Libellus de Alchimia* (ascribed to Albertus Magnus) Virginia Heines (trs.), University of California Press, 1958, p. 22.</small>

Psychology now calls this love in the heart of the lion compulsive projection. The alchemical basis of this kind of projection is actually the sulphur in the heart that does not recognize it is imagining. The objective *himma* is literalized into the objects of its desire. Imagination is thrown outwards, ahead of itself; and the task is less to take back these kinds of projections – who takes them back and where are they put – but more to leap after the projectile[11] reclaiming it as imagination, thereby recognizing that himma demands that images always be experienced as sensuous independent bodies.[12] There are styles of projection: it is not a unitary mechanism. Cordial projection requires an equally leonine mode of consciousness: pride, magnanimity, courage. To desire and to see through desire – this is the courage that the heart requires.

As Jung says: "Sulphur represents the active substance of the sun... the motive factor in consciousness, on the one hand will and on the other compulsion" (*CW 14*: § 151).[13] Compulsion becomes will through courage; it is in the heart that the operations upon sulphur are performed. We shall come back to these operations in the second part. For now it is enough to recognize compulsive projection to be a necessary activity of the sulphur, as the way in which this heart thinks, where thought and desire are one.

The unitary, wholehearted thought of this heart presents psychology with an animal mode of reflection. This reflection – in which imagination and perception, thinking and feeling, self and world are one – is not a bending back, after the event and away from

11  I borrow this thought from Wolfgang Giegerich, "Der Sprung nach dem Wurf – Über das Einholen der Projektion und den Ursprung der Psychologie", *Gorgo I*, 1979, pp. 49–71.

12  Sulphur, according to Paracelsus (I:245) "gives body, substance, and build" to the imagination of alchemy. The "body which is appropriate to each it takes from sulphur." "Body" of course has many meanings depending on the alchemist and the context of operation, but here I take body to mean *soma* as in ancient Greek usage like what we would now call "physical person" (cf. Hirzel, *op. cit. inf.*).

13  The works of Jung quoted are *The Collected Works of C. G. Jung*, Bollingen Series, Princeton Univ. Press and Routledge & Kegan Paul (London) = *CW*.; *Memories, Dreams, Reflections* recorded and edited by Aniela Jaffé, London: Collins and Routledge & Kegan Paul, 1963 = *MDR*.

it. Instead, the reflection occurs with the perception as its sheen and luster, the play of *its* lights rather than the light of consciousness I bring to it, each thing immediately reflecting its image in the perceiving heart; mental reflection foreshortened to animal reflex.

The animal heart directly intends, senses, and responds as a unitary whole. Wholeness in the act, as a quality of the act. This heart we find first elaborated in Aristotle who described it as the hottest bodily part (493a3, 743b27, 744a29) and the central source of our blood and our organic heat (667b17, 665b32, 766b1). It senses and responds directly, for the organs that sense the world run to the heart (781a21, 647a25ff, 703b24, 743b26), and especially taste[14] and touch provide this immediate connection of the heart with the world.

Aristotle's formulation of the *cœur de lion* in his physiology of perception compares with that of the Paracelsians. They conceived the microcosmic heart in our breasts to be the place of imagining, which imagination conforms with the macrocosmic heart of the world, the sun. The animal heart here bespeaks the animal sun there in an animated world.[15] The world is a place of living images and our hearts are the organ that tell us so.

If the heart is the place of images, a heart infarction refers to a heart stuffed (*farctus* = stuffed, crammed, filled, fattened) with its products, imaginings. It is clogged by its own sulphuric riches that have not gone into circulation. Either they have been constrained by narrowings and not been allowed passage, or they have been seen only as literal actions-in-the-world, instead of also as imaginings of the heart, belonging to its interior circulation. This same literalism of the heart's sulphur returns in the very theories of heart disease, where fat, narrowing of circulation, deed-in-the-world reappear as

14 Sulphur is responsible for "The Tastes and Odours of Metals" in Albertus Magnus, *Book of Minerals*, Dorothy Wyckoff (trs.), Oxford: Clarendon, 1967, pp. 194–95.

15 Cf. Allen G. Debus, *The English Paracelsians*, London: Oldbourne, 1965, pp. 113–116 on Fludd's sun as the "heart of heaven" and the heart as the sun of the body, connected by 'air' and in circulation both in the macrocosm and the microcosm of the blood.

explanations. Then we are attacked by our own lion in the breast, our heart full of himma, whose "magna flamma" insists that *enthymesis* never cease, that each particular throb of the heart be recognized as a thought of the heart.

## *The Heart of Harvey*

Harvey's volume on the heart, 72 quarto pages in Latin, printed in Frankfurt in 1628 when Harvey was 50 years old, is called (in English translation) "An Anatomical Dissertation concerning the Motion of the Heart and Blood in Animals". Its key idea, presented with meticulous verification and excellent reasoning, had already been recorded by him as early as 1616 in notes for lectures given in London at the College of Physicians. In these notes he states that the "perpetual motion of the blood in a circle is brought about by the beat of the heart".[16]

The motion of the blood in a circle is an archetypal idea. Similar depictions have been attributed to Huang-ti in China[17] in the third millenia before our era and deduced from Egyptian papyrus of the Old Kingdom.[18] Besides, Fludd, Cesalpino, Servetus, da Vinci and Valverde have each good reason to be called forerunners of Harvey. Giordano Bruno wrote (*De Rerum Principiis*, 16 March 1590): "... the blood in the animal body moves in a circle in order to distribute

16 "Perpetuum sanguinis motum in circulo fieri pulsu cordis." Cf. Ch. Singer, *The Discovery of the Circulation of the Blood*, London: Dawson, 1956.
17 Felix Boenheim, *Von Huang-ti bis Harvey*, Jena: Fischer Verlag, 1957; T. Doby, *Discoverers of Blood Circulation*, N.Y.: Abelard-Schuman, 1963.
18 Ibid. The "thought of the heart" can be expressed in more ideographic languages such as Chinese *Hsin-li* as heart-reason; Hebrew *leb* as heart-imagination or intelligence; and Egyptian *ab* which means "interior, sense, intelligence, understanding, attention, intention, manner, will, wish, desire, mind, courage, lust, and self" [compare Greek *enthymesis*] according to E. A. Wallis Budge, *An Egyptian Hieroglyphic Dictionary*, N.Y.: Dover, 1978, 1:37b. Unlike other principal organs, the heart was not eviscerated in the preparation of the Egyptian mummy for the underworld, but was left in the cadaver.

its motor."[19] In Act I, Scene 1 of *Coriolanus*, Shakespeare's play conventionally dated 1609, compact with words such as "state" and "honour" and in which we find images of lions, courage, rage and anger, proudness and nobility, we also find this metaphor of the blood's circulation (moving from a central organ): "I send it through the rivers of your blood, even to the court, the heart, to the seat of the brain; / And, through the cranks and offices of man, / The strongest nerves and small inferior veins / From me receive that natural competency / Whereby they live."[20] Circulation of the blood was in the *Zeitgeist* of the early seventeenth century.

Harvey still maintains the archetypal images of our first heart, that of the King. His little book opens with a dedication to Charles the First, comparing the King in his Kingdom with the heart in the midst of the body; and the book concludes with this passage: "...the heart like a prince in a kingdom, in whose hands lie the chief and highest authority, rules overall; it is the original and foundation from which all power is derived, on which all power depends in the animal body."[21] But Harvey's heart differs essentially from that older heart of lion and feeling, because his is a heart of visible demonstration. Harvey tells how the valves work, how the chambers and veins function. His crucial demonstration that the blood must circulate combines visible evidence (ligature of blood vessels so as to show the differences between veins and arteries) and quantitative mensuration. If the pulse, he asks, beats 72 times a minute, in one hour the left ventricle will throw into the aorta no less than $72 \times 60 \times 2$ or 8640 ounces of blood, that is, 38 stone 8 pounds, which is three times the weight of a heavy man! Where can all this blood come from? Where can it all go to? It must be the same blood in continuous circulation, leaving the heart and returning to it. And

19 The Bruno and Shakespeare examples are also quoted by F. Marti-Ibanez, "Padua and London: A Harveian Tale of Two Cities", *Centaur*, New York: M.D. Publ., 1958.
20 The word "heart" appears in 39 lines in *Coriolanus*; more frequently than in *Othello, Hamlet, Julius Caesar, Romeo and Juliet,* or *Henry V* – though not more often than in *King Lear, Richard II* or *Antony and Cleopatra*.
21 Singer, *op. cit.*, p. 66.

# The Thought of the Heart

how does this heart work? Like a water bellows, he says; our pulse is a pump.[22] What pounds in our ears, throbs in our groins, is the beat of a machine.

Hold it in your hands, he explains: "...it may be felt to become harder during its action. This hardness proceeds from tension, just as when the forearm is grasped, its muscles... become tense and firm when [these muscles] move the fingers... during action the heart... becomes erect, hard and smaller... the movement is plainly of the same nature as that of the muscles when they contract." (1–2 "Anatomical Dissertation")

This is all new: this hardness of the heart, this smallness, this muscular tense heart, inherently stressed, this pumping machine, demonstrated so directly and tangibly – hold it in your hands. We can take the heart in our hands. As my friend in Dallas, the phenomenologist Robert Romanyshyn, has indicated in his lectures about Harvey's vision, the scientific outlook requires the kind of heart it sees. The act of demonstration creates what it demonstrates. An invisible heart of himma and the courageous heart of the lion cannot be held in the hand, nor can the volume of their sanguinity be computed.

The approach to the heart by means of literal sense perception creates the mechanical heart that Harvey describes. Himma is at work even in science – indeed in scientific thought perhaps more than anywhere – because what is imagined by science is presented as if objectively real and independent of a subjective imagination. The scientific imagination is himma literalized.

With Harvey, we are not only in the new scientific age; we are in a new world-order where the lion no longer rules. The end of the animal kingdom, the kingship of and kinship with the animal. Our animal selves become symbolic lore or history or evolution, but no longer actual and present; Harvey's praise for Aristotle, Galen and Fabricius, and the King too, is now only tribute to the past and the great. The heart as the King is now a pretty way of speaking, a conceit. The past is a rhetorical flourish appropriate to opening and

---
22 Singer, *op. cit.*, p. 46

closing a book, but incidental to its body – and our body. Tradition has now become history, history of medicine, as if the heart were not the same heart, always. Let us take note: the evisceration of tradition takes place when the heart loses its relation with organic nature, its empathy with all things, when the core of our breast moves from an animal to a mechanical imagination.

When the great tradition becomes only the past from which we evolve, then the stage is set for Darwin and the progressive evolution away from the animal. Descartes, La Mettrie – the animal as machine. And the stage is set for the end of the divine rightness of Kings and the new kingdom of man, humanism. The heart itself shifts from royal rule to the common heart of sentiment, the fraternity of feeling that accompanies the machine as its counterpart.

The transfiguration of our Western culture into an industrial egalitarianism with materialistic values first required Harvey's transformation of the heart. The king had first to become a machine, and the machine become a spare part, interchangeable from any chest to any other. Of course, the heart soon reacted: already by 1654 Pascal was converted to the heart of faith and feeling, and in 1673 Margarite-Marie Alacoque, since sainted, began her series of extraordinary visions on which is based the Catholic doctrine of the Sacred Heart. The Feast was allowed a hundred years later, in 1765, just after Rousseau published *Émile*.

History is psychology because tradition is always going on in the soul. The mechanical heart and the sentimental heart still imply each other, still require each other, and neither remembers the lion.

Today, each of us carries the Harveyein heart in our breasts: My heart is a pump. It has thick muscular walls that need exercise. If it fails, I put in a pacemaker or some by-pass tubing. If it wears out, irreparably, I can let that heart doctor, named paradoxically enough, Christian Barnard, remove it and replace it with a spare – an operation, by the way, already presaged by St. Catherine of Siena who prayed and was vouchsafed that prayer that her heart be removed and that of the Saviour placed in her breast.

# The Thought of the Heart

To keep my ticker running, I jog it. The heart must be lean, trim, erect, so I watch for extremes of intensity, like idle leisure, and of abuse, like passionate excitement. Now, the heart is no longer the animal of love and heat, the place of *himma*, throbbing out its imaginative forms. Now, its signals are decoded into little messages about life-expectancy. For my heart can insult me, attack me. I must propitiate it: I take this for my heart, do that for my heart, watch out for my heart. I turn it in regularly for a check-up. The mechanical model, by means of which I watch the heart as if it were a dead thing outside me, moves with technological progress from Harvey's water-bellows, to the stethoscope, to the ECG attached to me by wires, my heart on a TV screen. Our modes of imagining its conservation are also mechanical: unobstructed elastic channels, light viscosity of the blood, reduced pressure of blood volume against arterial walls.

The heart is still king, still the pace-maker, but now a tyrant, for heart and circulatory diseases are "the number one killers", usually striking in the night. It cannot be trusted; we cannot have faith in the very organ which once was the source of faith. The heart has become my enemy, my killer, my death.

The dead heart was born into Western consciousness, according to Romanyshyn, at that moment when Harvey conceived the heart to be divided. He saw, down its middle, separating left from right, an impassable wall. Because of this impassable wall, the blood must necessarily be pumped through the great and complicated circulation through the lungs and entire body in order to move to the other side of the heart.[23] Hence, it is the divided heart that makes possible the *circulatio*.

Thus Harvey confirmed Ibn Sina's notion that 'heart' is a force occupying the whole body, the visible organ of which is the

[23] "It is important to remember that there is no communication between... one side of the heart and the... other side of the heart, except through the blood vessels and capillaries. [Capillaries were discovered by Malpighi only after Harvey's work.] The existence of a more direct means of communication was firmly believed until the seventeenth century... The removal of this belief was one of the most important events in the history of science." Singer, op. cit., p. 6. Harvey

anatomical heart.[24] And curiously, the circulation of the blood depended even as a scientific idea on a radical confirmation of the *cor duplex*, a heart divided against itself. Here, Harvey affirmed an archetypal idea that the heart is not simple, not one, but is inherently divided against itself, its left and right chambers, though side by side, are most remote to each other, without communication. We shall have to return to this innate *dipsychos*, or duplicity of the heart, later. For it was here, I believe, in the visible demonstration of the inherent duplicity of the heart that the telling blow was struck against the naive cœur de lion and its faith in wholeheartedness. No longer could the world be one, under one rule of sun, king, and lion. The immediacy of action became doubled into complicated reflection. Thought lost its heart, heart its thought. The king was dead, and a wall had now been set between the world out there and subjective feelings in here, because even in the center of the breast there was division.

## *The Heart of Augustine*

More than the lion and the pump, it is the heart of Augustine that has most affected psychology, both as a field of thought and as everyday life where heart means feeling, my own interior nature, the secret chamber of my person. As Dietrich von Hildebrand[25] says:

> It is the heart which is the most intimate part of a person, the core, the real self... (p. 109). It is in the heart that the secret of the person is to be found, it is here that the most intimate word is spoken (p. 97).

Another Catholic philosopher, Paul Henry[26], says it was Augustine

> demonstrated the wall down the middle in a late experiment on – N.B. – the corpse of a hanged highwayman, and described it in a letter to a colleague. Doby, *op. cit.*, pp. 219–200.

24 See below note 65.
25 *The Sacred Heart*, Baltimore: Helicon, 1965.
26 *Saint Augustine on Personality*, N.Y.: Macmillan, 1960, p. v.

who "first came into prominence and undertook an analysis of the philosophical and psychological concepts of person and personality". And the Protestant theologian Adolf von Harnack said:

> "Where in all the history of the Western Church do we encounter a man whose influence is comparable to the influence of Saint Augustine?"[27]

I wish to impress upon you Augustine's importance in developing the philosophy of the personal feeling heart in order that we recognize that the contemporary cult of feeling as the 'true' thought of the heart is fundamentally Augustinian Christianity. We cannot confront the personalism of California without first passing through the confessionalism of Carthage.

Augustine's thought of the heart begins with his *Confessions*. This book is a testament of interior experience, the first book of psychology developing an idea of person as experiencing subject. Person is a word that the Greeks did not have, nor does the word appear in the Greek New Testament.[28] Augustine's use of the word *cor*, heart, equates it with *intima mea*, inward dwelling, "closet" (*En. Ps.* CXLII [2]), the anima or soul ("our shared bedroom, my heart" – *Conf.* 8.8).

Heart is essentially *my* heart: "Cor meum, ubi ego sum quicumque sum – my heart, where I am, whatever I am" (*Conf.* 10.3). It is the deepest place, an unfathomable "abyss" (one of his favorite words for heart), in which my truth resides: "... whose heart is seen into? What he is engaged on, what he is inwardly capable of, what he is inwardly doing or purposing, what he is inwardly wishing to happen, or not to happen, who shall comprehend?" (*En. Ps.* XLII 12 or XLI 8 [12].) Already, a psychoanalysis of feelings. Heart as inwardness – not as lion, sun, king of the body in conformity with the world.

Feelings are the way of knowing this heart and confession brings

---

27 From von Hildebrand, *op. cit.*
28 Cf. Rudolf Hirzel, *Die Person, Begriff und Name derselben im Altertum*, Königlich Bayerische Akademie der Wissenschaft, München 1914.

it to expression.[29] The thought of the heart is feeling: "Where the heart is, there is either blessedness or misery" (*De. mus.* 6.11). This heart is emotional, the place of storms and tears, of conflict, of *Gemüt* in its fullest sense: "Arise, seek, sigh, pant with longing, knock at what is shut. If we do not yet long, not yet sigh, we shall only be casting pearls... Therefore, dearest beloved, I would stir up longing in your heart" *(In Joann. ev. 18.7).*

Let us notice at once that this intimate heart of feelings is not the heart of the Greeks, or of the Hebrews[30], or of the Persian thought presented by Corbin. Corbin (*CI*: 221&n) states quite clearly that the heart's characteristic action is not feeling, but sight. Love is of the spirit, quickening the soul to its images in the heart. The heart is not so much the place of personal feeling as it is the place of true imagining, the *vera imaginatio* that reflects the imaginal world in the microcosmic world of the heart. Feelings stir as images move. Hence one has recourse to the heart – not because it is where the truth of feelings resides or where one feels one's personal soul. No. One turns to the heart because here is where the essences of reality are presented by the imaginal to the imagination. The passionate spirit of himma that moves through the heart is not the *passio* of personal confessional life.

Now we see what happens to the imagination in a heart of personal feeling. By personalizing the heart and locating there the word of God, the imagination is driven into exile. Its place is usurped by dogma, by images already revealed. Imagination is driven into the lower exile of sexual fantasy, the upper exile of metaphysical conception, or the outer exile of objective data, none of which reside in the heart and all of which therefore seem heartless, mere instinct,

---

29 Cf. Robert Meagher, *An Introduction to Augustine*, N.Y.: Harper Colophon, 1978, Chapter "Person", rich with passages from Augustine that link confession of feeling with personhood. Also, A. Maxsein, "*Philosophia cordis* bei Augustinus", in *Augustinus Magister*, Études Augustiniennes Suppl. (Congrès Internat. Augustinien, Sept. 1954 (n.d.) I:357–71.

30 The shadings of difference are exposed by A. Guillaumont, "Les sens des noms du cœur dans l'antiquité", *Le Cœur* – Études Carmélitaines, Bruges: Desclée de Brouwer, 1950, pp. 41–81.

sheer speculation, brute fact. When imagination is driven out, there remains only subjectivity – the heart of Augustine.

And this heart of subjective feeling holds imagination in its captivity. We judge our images in terms of their feelings. Whether a project or reverie be imagined further is determined by how it feels. Is this dream good or bad – feeling will tell you. To test something in the heart has come to mean what we feel about it, and to weigh the heart refers no longer to the gravity and substance of its images, but mainly to our personal motivations and reactions that can be discovered in confessional introspection.

A gulf opens between subjective feelings without imaginative forms, and the literalism of images as sensations, ideas, data without subjectivity. They do not confess; only I can confess. So anything they might say must be my projections. The whole endeavour of retrieving projections – that major enterprise of analytical practice – could become irrelevant once the theory of the heart were to shift from its personalistic base. We would then recognize much of what we call projection to be an attempt by the psyche to experience things beyond ourselves as imaginal presences, an attempt to restore both heart and image to things. Pornography, intellectual abstractions, and the impersonal data from the sciences and histories can be recovered by our taking them to heart, allowing them to invent themselves further, encouraging them to confess *their* imaginal reality.

It sounds as if our modern personalism of the heart, which we are attributing to Augustine, better belongs to Rousseau. It is Rousseau who wrote in his *Confessions*: "One must know how to analyze properly the human heart to disentangle the true feelings of nature", who also wrote there of Mme. de Warens' heart as her guide through the maze of feelings, and who, in his famous phrase from *Émile* – "Exister pour nous, c'est sentir" (*Émile*, pp. 252–53) – gives to the heart the rule by which all life can be measured.

Whether Augustine or Rousseau is the originator is less the issue than is the *confessional mode*. As Paul Henry says: "Augustine, interested in man, self, personality, thereby invented a new literary genre" (p. 12). This genre is the exposition of subjectivity, the confession, and it requires a rhetoric of the ego, the first person singular. Augustine says:

> Accept the books of my Confessions... There see me... there believe, not others about me, but myself; there mark me, and see what I was in myself, by myself... (*Ep. ad Darium* [Ep. 231]).

The word "confession" from *fassus* bears the root *pha* (Grk) and *bha* (Skr), "show", "light", "shine". It is the confessional literary genre of showing, not Augustine or Rousseau, which creates the experience of the heart as abyss, of experience as unfathomable, one's person a closet of deep interior darkness. This same genre also creates 'Augustine' and 'Rousseau' as necessary figures of the mode, heroes of the psychological. They are first person singulars, the feeling, suffering personalities, who perform the heroic task of bringing light out of their personal abyss. As soon as we start to confess, we enter this genre, and then we must struggle with finding the true 'me' hidden in the closet of personal feelings.

Here, confessional psychology literalizes the notion of revelation as a bringing to show what therefore must be concealed, light out of darkness, subjective heroics. Confessional psychology misses the fact that I am already revealed in my *Selbst-Darstellung*. Revelation already given with existence – not a task. Every move we make, phrase we utter, is confession of our heart because it reveals our images. Heart is manifest in the fantasies displayed in my life, not only concealed in my depths. In this way, confessional psychology subtly devalues the presentation of self in everyday life which for Augustine belongs anyway merely to the "exterior".

The truths of the heart do not have to be stated or even experienced as *my* feeling. When Empedocles (Frg. 115) describes the wandering, tormented souls in exile, and even confesses himself among these ("In that brood I too am numbered now"), it is a statement of the elements, an elemental statement about all souls, not a confession of his own life and heart. When Aristotle discusses catharsis and tragedy, or the nature of friendship and of courage, it is of all humans, an archetypal reflection, requiring no subject to the sentence, no rhetorical ego. When Sophocles presents the feelings of the heart in Oedipus, Antigone, Electra, or Philoctetes, these are figures of the imaginal whose dramas are staged in also my heart which mirrors macrocosmic life.

The heart can be disentangled from confessional personalism. We can be moved powerfully without confessing these movements to be our own. Empedocles, Aristotle, and Sophocles provide examples of the tragic, mythic mode of affective detachment. Another mode is the *récit*, or recitation, such as we find collected in Corbin's writings.

The difference between the confession and the recitation lies precisely in coming to a new realization of "experience". Confession confines experience to 'my' experience – what is registered in my nature. As long as experience means personal felt-experience, it requires the genre of confession, whether in depth psychology or in the arts, as subjectivism, expressionism, and personal romanticism. Feelings become crucial: my feelings *are* my heart. To discover its thought, I must reveal just what I feel.

The *récit*, however, is an account of events experienced, rather than of my experiencing. It was then unfolded; the angel then said; a mountain, a room, a colored light, a figure shone in splendour.[31] Like a walk through the world, there is this and this and this; the colors and shapes of the things illumined, their faces, is the confession – it is *their* coming to light, *their* testament, and *their* individuation, as Corbin said, not mine. The angel before the feeling he brings. Feelings are accessory to them, received from them. They are "divine influxes", as Blake said, moving through the heart in the company of images.

The *récit* also breaks up that identification with experience which confession reinforces: confession as possession, *my* sins. What I confess to, I must believe as truth, as history. "I did this, felt that,

---

[31] Examples of recitals fill Corbin's works; see especially his *Avicenna and the Visionary Recital* (2nd printing), Irving, Tx.: Spring Publ., 1980, and *L'archange empourpré*, Paris: Fayard, 1976.

wished and wanted." But ever since Freud we know that what goes on in the heart is neither truth nor history; it is desire and imagination. So, confession raises the problem of *Wahrheit* and *Dichtung*. Whenever we attempt to tell our feelings – what I really feel, what was my true motive – a certain duplicity starts up. Truth or fiction? We are in the midst of Harvey's *cor duplex*: we waver at the very moment we own up.

Again the problem is rhetorical: the first person singular implies a single feeling. The reporter is singular whereas the feelings are multiple. So, to get to the heart's core, we become fanatically confessional, intensely personal, letting it all show forth in order to get to this fictional, rhetorical 'true inside real feeling me'.

Confession supports one of our most cherished Western dogmas as Gilbert Durand and David Miller here have both said: the idea of a unified experiencing subject vis-a-vis a world that is multiple, disunited, chaotic. The first person singular, that little devil of an I – who, as psychoanalysis long ago has seen is neither first, nor a person, nor singular – is the confessional voice, imagining itself to be the unifier of experience. But experience can also be unified by the style in which it is enacted, by the images which form it, by its repetitive thematics, and by the relations amid which it unfolds. It does not have to be owned to be held. The heart in the breast is not your heart only: it is a microcosmic sun, a cosmos of all possible experiences that no one can own.

This problem of the experiencing subject holding the world together is not merely a language game, the grammar of the first personal singular creating ontology. It is more seriously a confessional ontology of the personalistic heart dominating our grammar, persuading us by our very sentence structures that when our pronoun is singular then so must be our verbs; our actions too must be single. The subject/predicate construction holds apart 'I' and everything else; whatever is not I becomes predicated of the subject. Imagine: we feel in such a way that this I, this me, is separate and over against the huge full world, as if a pair of equal co-ordinates.

In the practice of religion, confession is immediately followed by prayer. Recognition and repentance is not therapeutic enough; confession corrects personal experience, but does not remove us from it. Augustine recognized that confession becomes mere autobiography unless it is as well a devotion to the divine in the heart. Rousseau, too, located his divinity, "nature", in the heart, which gives to both their confessions the testimony of religion.

Psychotherapy stops short. It invites confession but omits prayer. The religious impulse is provoked and then unsatisfied. A secondary religious aura then pervades many aspects of psychotherapy. Analysis itself is regarded religiously; "experience" is endowed with religious values, becoming sacred, unavailable to examination: the dogma of experience. The emotions of the heart are taken for religious revelations.

Confession is an initiatory stage of psychotherapy, as Jung said (*CW 4*: §§ 431–35; *12*: § 3; *16*: § 153). But because it fails to carry beyond itself, confession turns therapy into an addictive repetition. Rather than releasing images to flow to and from the heart as independent realities, confession fixes them there. The image is imprisoned in its feeling, rather than the feeling released into its images.

Prayer offers a therapy of confession. By praying we move out. As Coleridge[32] insisted, the intensity of Western subjectivism requires a personal divinity to whom we address our hearts. We are saved by these divinities, psychologically, for we are saved from the personalism of feeling by bringing those feelings to persons who are not we, who are beyond our notion of experience. They who are

---

32 Coleridge who invented the term "self-realization" saw that this self of personality becomes only self-seeking subjectivism unless its ground was 'outside' itself in a 'person' that is not the human person and to whom prayer was addressed. (A. J. Harding, *Coleridge and the Idea of Love*, Cambridge Univ. Press, 1974, p. 143; L. S. Lockridge, *Coleridge the Moralist*, Cornell Univ. Press, pp. 124–26.) His own immense problems with prayer – and with his creative imagination – perhaps are linked because he did not accept the intercessory figures which are so essential to the notion of prayer in Corbin as a dialogical encounter with such figures. Coleridge could never release prayer from moral duty to a single high God into prayer as imagination. (Cf. Lockridge, pp. 102–109; J. R. Barth, *Coleridge and Christian Doctrine*, Harvard Univ. Press, 1969, pp. 181–85.

they. They who give experience and are its ground, so that the himma in the heart recognizes them, and not ourselves, as the true Persons. We talk to them, they to us[33]; and this "dialogical situation" (*CI*: 247) which constitutes prayer (in distinction to worship, idolatry, ecstasy) as a psychological act is, in Corbin's words (*CI*: 248), "the supreme act of the Creative Imagination".

By means of such prayer, the heart can move from those limited persons and powers – the dialogical situation of the analyst and the patient, their mutual feelings, their transferences. Secular therapy has transferred onto these human figures and the movements of their hearts the imaginal figures of prayer. Transference is the ultimate consequence of secularized confession, and the resolution of transference, as Jung said, is a religious care with the impersonal, the persons of the imaginal. Transference, the mystery of therapy, can be moved only when we move the heart from its confessional mode of experiencing to a prayerful response to its images – witnessing; Corbin's *récit*.

The response to these persons begins in an activated imagination, in himma, the heart's ardent witness to imaginal persons independent of the heart which beholds them. Not held; beheld, and we beholden to powers, we in their luminosity, watched by them, guarded, remembered; visible presences, enlightening our darkness by their beauty.

## II. THE HEART OF BEAUTY

When Petrarca, age 22, in the Church of Santa Chiara at Avignon, on April 6th, 1327, caught sight of a lovely girl, his heart pounded or stopped or leapt into his throat. His soul had been assailed by beauty. Was this when the Renaissance began? Or had it already begun, this Vita Nuova, when Dante, in 1274 at the age of nine first

---

33 Examples of such talks in active imagination were presented in detail at *Eranos 46–1977* in my paper "Psychotherapy's Inferiority Complex".

saw Beatrice ("she who confers blessing"), crimson-dressed girl-child and anima mundi, awakening his heart to the aesthetic life.

"At that moment," writes Dante, "I say... the spirit of life, which hath its dwelling in the secretest chamber of the heart, began to tremble so violently that the least pulses of my body shook; and in trembling it said these words: 'Here is a deity stronger than I; who, coming, shall rule over me.'" (*Vita Nuova*, II) From then on he was a devotee of this deity in the shape of his soul figure, dedicated to love, imagination, and poetic beauty, all three inseparably.

These couples, Petrarca and Laura, Dante and Beatrice, had no personal satisfaction, no human relationship. Yet what emerged from these happenings in the heart was the transformation of all Western culture, commencing as an aesthetic transformation; it was generated by Beauty. Was not Psyche in the Apuleius tale singled out by her beauty, and is not Aphrodite, the Beautiful One, the soul of the universe (*psyché tou kosmou* or *anima mundi*) that produces the perceptible world according to Plotinus (III, 5, 4) and also the soul of each of us?

Can we attend to what these figures and tales are saying? Can we realize that we are each, in soul, children of Aphrodite, that the soul is a *therapeutes*, as was Psyche, in the temple of Venus – *that* is where it is in devotion. The soul is born in beauty and feeds on beauty, requires beauty for its life. If we read Plato the way Plotinus did, and understand Psyche the way Apuleius did, and experience soul as did Petrarca and Dante, then *psyche is the life of our aesthetic responses,* that sense of taste in relation with things, that thrill or pain, disgust or expansion of breast, those primordial aesthetic reactions of the heart are soul itself speaking. Psyche's first trait and the way we know her first, is neither by her labours, the *work* of soul-making, nor by her sufferings for love, nor in her oppression in lostness, the absence and deprivation of soul – these in the Apuleian tale all come later. We know her first by her primary characteristic given with her nature: Psyche is beautiful.

How is it possible that beauty has played such a central and obvious part in the history of the soul and its thought, and yet is absent in modern psychology? Imagine – eighty years of depth psychology without a thought to beauty! Even now psychology tends to reduce the aesthetic from its primacy to a diagnostic attribute, "aestheticism".[34] Those tales of Petrarca and Dante become anima fascinations, immature idealizations of repression, unrelated narcissism, typically puer aestheticizing.

We have taken Psyche's beauty only symbolically as meaning something other than itself. We have not read carefully what Apuleius says, nor placed it against his Platonic background. Else we would have understood that Psyche's beauty was visible, sensate[35], as Laura's was to Petrarca, as Aphrodite shows herself nude. Moreover, in our psychological interpretations of Psyche (Neumann, von Franz, Hillman, Ulanov[36]) we have mistaken her beauty as a mere motif to be understood, rather than as the essential characteristic of Psyche's image, a mistake which requires a new reading of the tale in terms of the soul's essentially aesthetic nature.

If beauty is not given full place in our work with psyche, then the soul's essential realization cannot occur. And, a psychology that does not start in aesthetics – as Psyche's tale starts in beauty and as Aphrodite is the *psyché tou kosmou* or soul in all things – cannot claim to be truly psychology since it omits this essential trait of the soul's nature. We are led already to see that a full depth psychology expressing the nature of Psyche must also be a depth aesthetics. Further, if we would recuperate the lost soul, which is after all the main aim of all depth psychologies, we must recover our lost aesthetic reactions, our sense of beauty.

34 Cf. Jung, CW 7: § 167.
35 Cf. Apuleius, *The Golden Ass*, Book VI:28, where Psyche's beauty is essential to her nature and immediately visible to all people in the street, the very trait that made Venus envious.
36 Cf. E. Neumann, *Amor and Psyche*, N.Y.: Pantheon, 1956; J. Hillman, *The Myth of Analysis*, N.Y.: Harper & Row, 1978; M.-L. von Franz, *A Psychological Interpretation of the Golden Ass of Apuleius*, Dallas: Spring Publ., 1980; A. B. Ulanov, *The Feminine in Jungian Psychology and Christian Theology*, Evanston: Northwestern Univ. Press, 1971.

So, in this hour we shall be entering another mode of the heart's thought, an exegesis of the heart that might lead it and us from the captivity in the modes we previously examined. Our theme is the thought of the heart as the aesthetic response.

By beauty we do not mean beautifying, adornments, decorations. We do not mean aesthetics as a minor branch of philosophy concerned with taste, form and art criticism. We do not mean "disinterestedness" – the lion asleep. Nor can beauty be held in museums, by maestros at the violin, a profession of artists. Indeed we must cleave beauty altogether away from art, art history, art objects, art appreciation, art therapy. These are each positivisms: that is, they posit beauty into an instance of it: they position *aisthesis* in aesthetic events such as beautiful objects.

In pursuing what we mean by beauty we are obstructed by the word beauty itself. It strikes the ear as so effete, so ineffectual, lovely and etheric, so far removed from the soul's desperate concerns. Again we see how our notions are determined by archetypal patterns, as if beauty had become relegated only to Apollo, the examination of invisible forms like music, belonging to collectors and subject to disputes in journals of aesthetics. Or, beauty has been given over wholly to the soft hands of Adonis and Paris, beauty as violets, mutilation and death. In Plato and Plotinus, however, beauty does not have this glabrous, passive and ungenerative sense at all, and it is rarely brought into relation with art. In fact beauty is not 'beautiful' and Socrates' person is witness. Rather, the beautiful in Platonic thought can only be understood if we can enter an Aphroditic cosmos and this in turn means penetrating into the ancient notion of *aisthesis* (sense-perception) from which aesthetics derives.

We must press beyond our usual ideas of beauty that have held the imagination captive to heavenly notions only, Aphrodite Urania, and away from the world of sense in which Aphrodite was always immanent. Hence, her nakedness has been pornographized by denigrating the visibility of physical appearance. As well, these lofty ideas have mystified revelation into an eschatological expectation: revelation comes as an epiphany that must shatter the sensate world only when we cannot sense the revelation in the immediate presentation of things as they are.

As Corbin writes (*ML*: 103): Beauty is that great category which specifically refers to the *Deus revelatus*, "the supreme theophany, divine self-revelation." As the Gods are given with creation so is their beauty in creation, and is the essential condition of *creation as manifestation*. Beauty is the manifest anima mundi – and do notice here it is neither transcendent to the manifest or hiddenly immanent within, but refers to appearances as such, created as they are, in the forms with which they are given, sense data, bare facts, Venus Nudata. Aphrodite's beauty refers to the luster of each particular event; its clarity, its particular brightness; that particular things appear at all and in the form in which they appear.

Beauty as Plato describes it in the *Phaedrus* (250b) is the manifestation, the showing forth of the hidden noumenal Gods and imperceptible virtues like temperance and justice. All these are but ideas, archetypes, pure forms, invisible didactic talk unless accompanied by beauty. "For beauty alone," he says, "this has been ordained, to be the most manifest to sense…" (250d). Beauty is thus the very sensibility of the cosmos, that it has textures, tones, tastes, that it is attractive. Alchemy might call this cosmic gloss, sulphur.

Here we must recall that *kosmos* originally in Greek was an aesthetic idea, and a polytheistic one. It referred to the right placing of the multiple things of the world, their ordered arrangement. Kosmos did not mean a collective, general, abstract whole. It did not mean universe, as turning around one point *(unus-verto)* or turned into one. This translation of cosmos into universe is a typical Roman imperialism unifying and obliterating the Greek particular sense of the world.

Kosmos also implied aesthetic qualities such as becomingly, decently, duly, honorably, creditably. "Cosmetics" is closer to the original meaning than is our word "cosmic" (as vast, unspecified, empty). *Kosmos* was used especially of women in respect to their embellishments; the Stoics used the word for the *anima mundi*.

That today "cosmic" has come to mean unimaginable and vague outer space only tells us further what has happened to Aphrodite Urania when severed from her sensate counterpart Pandemos.

If beauty is inherent and essential to soul, then beauty appears wherever soul appears. That revelation of soul's essence, the actual showing forth of Aphrodite in psyche, her smile[37], is called in mortal language, "beauty". All things as they display their innate nature present Aphrodite's goldenness; they shine forth and as such are aesthetic. Here, I am merely restating what Adolf Portmann has elaborated at Eranos for forty years: the idea of *Selbstdarstellung* (self-presentation) as the revelation to the senses of essential *Innerlichkeit* (interiority). Visible form is a show of soul. The being of a thing is revealed in the display of its *Bild* (image).

Beauty is not an attribute then, something beautiful, like a fine skin wrapped round a virtue; the aesthetic aspect of appearance itself. Were there no beauty, along with the good and the true and the one, we could never sense them, know them. Beauty is an *epistemological* necessity; it is the way in which the Gods touch our senses, reach the heart and attract us into life.[38]

As well, beauty is an *ontological* necessity, grounding the sensate particularity of the world. Without Aphrodite, the world of particulars becomes atomic particles. Life's detailed variety is called

---

37 Paul Friedrich, *The Meaning of Aphrodite*, Univ. of Chicago, 1978, pp. 202–04. "Through Aphrodite the whole world becomes pellucid and thus so brilliant and smiling...", K. Kerényi, *Goddesses of Sun and Moon*, Spring Publ., 1979, p. 58. Compare *SB*, 213: "The power of imagination is without doubt consubstantial with the soul... In fact, with respect to the soul, the Imagination is like the Soul of the Heaven of Venus." Both the sensible nature of imagination – that it is not merely abstract phantasms in the mind – and the imaginal, pellucid nature of sensation – that the world is not merely dense, concrete and unsmiling – we owe to Aphrodite.

38 As Walter F. Otto (*The Homeric Gods*, N.Y.: Pantheon, 1954, p. 101) points out, Aphrodite is not the desire of Eros proceeding "from the desiring subject, but from the beloved object. Aphrodite is not the loving one; she is beauty and smiling charm; she enraptures. Not the urge to take possession comes first, but rather the magic of an appearance that draws irresistibly..."

chaos, multiplicity, amorphous matter, statistical data. Such is the world of sense without Aphrodite. Then sense must be made of appearance by abstract philosophical means – which distorts philosophy itself from its true base.

If, as we said in Part I, philosophy takes rise in *philos*, it also refers to Aphrodite in another way. For *sophia* originally means the skill of the craftsman, the carpenter (*Iliad:* XV, 412) the seafarer (Hesiod, *Works:* 651), the sculptor (Aristotle, *Nic. Eth.*, vi: 1141a).[39] Sophia originates in and refers to the aesthetic hands of Daedalus and Hephaistos[40], who was of course conjoined with Aphrodite and so is inherent to her nature. With Aphrodite informing our philosophy, each event has its own smile on its face and appears in a particular mode, fashion, style. Aphrodite gives an archetypal background to the philosophy of "eachness" and the capacity of the heart to find "intimacy" with each particular event in a pluralistic cosmos (Wm. James).[41]

Now, the organ which perceives these faces is the heart. The thought of the heart is physiognomic. To perceive, it must imagine. It must see shapes, forms, faces – angels, demons, creatures of every sort in things of any kind; thereby the heart's thought personifies, ensouls, and animates the world. Petrarca sees Laura:

---

39 Aristotle recognizes the first meaning of *sophia*, referring to the *sophia* (skill in art) of Phidias and Polyclitus; but then he goes on to separate the term from its aesthetic base and give it the abstract sense of "knowledge of highest objects" and "truth about the first principles". Once *sophia* has been divided from aesthetic skill, the handcraft aspect returns as secondary in the very next paragraphs, e.g., *phronesis* or practical wisdom. This split between wisdom and practical action still detrimentally determines all later Aristotelian-influenced metaphysics, whereas *sophia* originally implies that thought and action lie together in any single move of the aesthetic hand.

40 Cf. Xenophon, *Memorabilia* 4, 2, 33; Plato, *Protagoras* 321d.

41 In his *A Pluralistic Universe* (Hibbert Lectures, 1909), William James argues for a radical pluralism of "eachness" against all varieties of rational and abstract monism. Essential to his argument is the experience of "intimacy" which he claims is only possible within a pluralistic universe. See his Chapters I and VIII, especially.

> ... in pathless forest shades,
> I see the face I fear, upon the bushes
> Or on an oaken trunk; or from the stream
> she rises; flashes on me from a cloud
> Or from clear sky; or issues from a rock, ...[42]

The lines are not *to* Laura, a love lyric, but a description of Laura, the soul personified, the figuration in the heart by means of which aesthetic perception proceeds. It brings to life things as forms that speak.

As we saw above, it was Aristotle's psychology that laid the basis for the connection between *aisthesis* and the heart. It may be strange to hear me speak in his praise, but there are many Aristotles, and my delight is in Aristotle the biologist who took the world of sense and shape to heart. In Aristotelian psychology, the organ of aisthesis is the heart, passages from all sense organs run to it; there the soul is "set on fire".[43] Its thought is innately aesthetic and sensately linked with the world.

This link between heart and the organs of sense is not simple mechanical sensationalism; it is aesthetic. That is, the activity of perception or sensation in Greek is *aisthesis* which means at root "taking in" and "breathing in" – a "gasp"[44], that primary aesthetic response.

Translators have turned *aisthesis* into "sense-perception", a British empiricist's notion, John Locke's sensation. But Greek "sense–

---

42  E. H. Wilkins, *The Life of Petrarch*, Univ. of Chicago, 1963, p. 20 (from *Metricae*, I, 6).

43  As discussed by Charles Lefevre in *Aristotle on the Mind and the Senses*, G. E. R. Lloyd and G. E. L. Owen (eds.), Cambridge Univ. Press, 1978, pp. 44–45.

44  R. B. Onians, *The Origins of European Thought*, Cambridge Univ. Press, 1954, pp. 74–75. Onians notes parallels with Hindu thought that speaks of the senses as breaths. Other parallels, deriving perhaps from Aristotle, occur in Avicenna (O. C. Gruner, *The Canon of Medicine of Avicenna*, London: Luzac, 1930, pp. 124): "The foundation or beginning of all these [soul] faculties is traceable to the heart", where "heart" means "a storehouse of the breath" (p. 123) which itself is "a luminous substance ... a ray of light" (p. 535).

perception" cannot be understood without taking into account the Greek Goddess of the senses or the organ of Greek sensation, the heart, and the root in the word – that sniffing, gasping, breathing in of the world.

What is it to 'take in' or breathe in the world? First, it means aspiring and inspiring the literal presentation of things by gasping. The transfiguration of matter occurs through wonder. This aesthetic reaction which precedes intellectual wonder inspires the given beyond itself, letting each thing reveal its particular aspiration within a cosmic arrangement.

Second, 'taking in' means taking to heart, interiorizing, becoming intimate with in an Augustinian sense. Not only *my* confession of my soul, but hearing the confession of the anima mundi in the speaking of things.

Third, 'taking in' means interiorizing the object into itself, into its image so that *its* imagination is activated (rather than ours), so that it shows its heart and reveals its soul, becoming personified and thereby lovable[45] – lovable not only to us and because of us, but because its loveliness increases[46] as its sense and its imagination unfold. Here begins phenomenology: in a world of ensouled phenomena. Phenomena need not be saved by grace or faith or all-embracing theory, or by scientific objectiveness or transcendental subjectivity. They are saved by the anima mundi, by their own souls and our simple gasping at this imaginal loveliness. The *ahh* of wonder, of recognition, or the Japanese *shee-e* through the teeth. The aesthetic response saves the phenomenon, the phenomenon which is the face of the world. "Everything shall perish except His face," says the Koran (xxxviii: 88) which Corbin can understand to mean "Every thing... except the Face of that thing" (*CI*: 244&n; *ML*: 112–13). God, the world, everything can pass into nothingness, victims of nihilistic constructions, metaphysical doubts, despairs of

---

45 On the relation of personification and loveableness, see my *Re-Visioning Psychology*, N.Y.: Harper & Row, 1975, pp. 14–16.
46 John Keats, *Endymion* (opening lines): "A thing of beauty is a joy forever: / Its loveliness increases; it will never / Pass into nothingness..."

every sort. What remains when all perishes is the face of things as they are. When there is nowhere to turn, turn back to the face before you, face the world. Here is the Goddess who gives a sense to the world that is neither myth nor meaning; instead that immediate thing as image, its smile, a joy, a joy that makes 'forever'.

### Kalon kagathon and Jung

The decline of Aphrodite from Queen of Soul, as in Plotinus' reading of the *Symposium*, "took more than a thousand years of Christian differentiation", says Jung. He writes (CW 9, i: § 60): "The anima believes in the *kalon kagathon*, the 'beautiful and the good', a primitive conception that antedates the discovery of the conflict between aesthetics and morals... The paradox of this marriage of ideas [beauty and goodness] troubled the ancients as little as it does the primitives. The anima is conservative and clings in the most exasperating fashion to the ways of earlier humanity."[47]

Jung usually gives good ear to "the ancients and the primitives". It is surprising to find him siding with the Christian position. Aestheticism, Jung says, is a cult of "refined hedonism" that "lacks all moral force" (CW 6: § 194); what seems a doctrine is mere anima prettiness which avoids the ugly. Again, we have the divided heart, an impenetrable wall between moral and aesthetic responses.

We need here to see more deeply into what anima is about in this marriage, for after all anima means soul and as Jung says (CW 9,i: § 60), "She is not a shallow creation." We need to remember that one of the archetypal persons within the anima of beauty is Aphrodite, whose conservative, instinctual reactions do not, cannot separate the aesthetic from the moral, and whose adherence to beauty rather than to ugliness requires an understanding of beauty, not in

---

47 The locus classicus of *kalon kagathon* is presented as a negative question in the *Hippias Major* 297c: "... should we be willing to say that the beautiful is not good, nor the good beautiful? Most certainly not."

the *fin de siècle* sense of Jung's education, but in the sense of the ancient and primitive, that polytheistic world of an earlier humanity in which the doctrine first took shape.

For beauty there, then, as we have just indicated, means the form of what is presented, that which is breathed in, *aisthesis*, and by which the value of each particular thing strikes the heart, the organ of aesthetic perception, where judgments are heartfelt responses, not merely critical, mental reflections. Reflection takes on another sense than our usual one. For the thought of the heart, reflection is not bending backward (*CW* 8: § 241), a movement afterwards in time, away from the object in space as it is transformed by psychic images and judged in the mind. Rather, reflection refers to the very aesthetic quality of any event, its sheen and shape, the luster of its skin. Event itself as image. An event reflects *itself* in its *Selbstdarstellung* as an image. Aesthetic reflection is immediately given with sensation, and the aesthetic response foreshortens reflection into reflex, the spontaneous reactions of the heart's taste.

Let us go back a moment to the biography of Jung. Two passages can help us understand Jung's view on beauty. The first is merely a scene. Little boy Jung in the eighteenth-century parsonage alone in a dark room in which was collected the art of the family. "Often I would sneak into that dark, sequestered room and sit for hours in front of the pictures, gazing at all this beauty. It was the only beautiful thing I knew" (*MDR*, p. 29). In the moral world of the parsonage, beauty was sequestered in a dark room into which one had to sneak. Morality and beauty cut apart: little boy Jung a result of the more than thousand-years Christian differentiation.

Moreover, beauty was positioned in *art* – paintings – the literalization of aesthesis in art objects.

The second biographical event occurs when Jung is painting and writing his fantasies. He asks himself:

> What am I really doing?... Whereupon a voice within me said, 'It is art.' I was astonished. It had never entered my head that what I was writing had any connection with art. Then I thought, 'Perhaps my unconscious is forming a personality that is not me, but which is insisting on coming through to expression.' I knew for

certainty that the voice had come from a woman. I recognized it as the voice of a patient, a talented psychopath who had a strong transference to me...

Obviously what I was doing wasn't science. What then could it be but art? It was as though these were the only alternatives in the world. That is the way a woman's mind works.

I said very emphatically to this voice that my fantasies had nothing to do with art, and I felt a great inner resistance. No voice came through, however, and I kept on writing. Then came the next assault, and again the same assertion: 'That is art.' This time I caught her and said, 'No, it is not art! On the contrary, it is nature', and prepared myself for an argument. When nothing of the sort occurred, I reflected that the 'woman within me' did not have the speech centres I had. And so I suggested that she use mine. She did so and came through with a long statement.

There are half a dozen things to note in this passage, which, let us remember, is precisely where Jung discovers "the woman within" and considers her to be soul or anima. This passage refers to the moment of the birth of "anima" in modern psychology, and anima's first statement is: Jung is doing art! Jung, however, identifies the voice with a "psychopathic patient" and attributes the opposition between art and science to "the way a woman's mind works". The opposition is his, and he is the one who resists, contradicts, and silences her; not she him. His reaction here is most unlike his close attention to Elijah and Philemon.[48]

Finally, her long statement, which presumably would sum up the anima's position on this crucial question as to what Jung was actually doing in his black and red books, his painting and writing of imaginations, is never given in the autobiography. How different Jung's first response to anima from that of Petrarca and Dante.

Had Jung listened more receptively to that voice of the soul – examples of which we presented at Eranos in 1977 – Jungian psychology might have taken a different tack: less division between aesthetics and science, aesthetics and nature, art and morality, less distrust of beauty and anima – and more sense for aesthetics.

We might better have understood that the soul, that "talented psychopath" who loved Jung, was the conserver of an archaic virtue

---

48 Cf. *Eranos 44-1975*, p. 417, where I discuss Jung's relation to these imaginal figures; Jung was however "distinctly suspicious" of Salome (*MDR*, p. 175), whom he met with Elijah and Philemon.

who *must* cling exasperatingly, because of resistance, to the doctrine of the beautiful and the good.

For, from the viewpoint of a psychology built from anima what we are doing when deeply engaged in imagination is indeed aesthetic. Depth psychology *is* a depth aesthetics, and the task of psychology from that date on would have been laying out the aesthetic modes of the deep imagination, rather than the examination of images in terms of comparisons with the natural science of physics, secular anthropology, moral symbols of religion, or practical considerations of medical therapeutics.

Jung justifies his suppression of her viewpoint upon the assumption that the aesthetic and the moral cannot be joined. He writes (p. 179): "If I had taken these fantasies... as art, they would have carried no more conviction than visual perceptions, as if I were watching a movie. I would have felt no moral obligation towards them." Soon afterwards he gives up what he calls the aestheticizing tendency in favour of the method of understanding (pp. 180–81; *CW 8*: §§ 172–79).

The separation of *kallos* from *agathon* degrades Aphrodite; she falls utterly into Aphrodite *pandemos,* a whore of sensuality without her heavenly counterpart. Then, the world of sense has no other than a sensuous claim; an image must be *understood* to be valued, so that we are obliged to *judge* our images morally, assign them a positive or negative value in order to know how to react. We have lost the response of the heart to what is presented to the senses. We find meanings and lose responses.

Psychology is still embroiled in this dilemma so vividly presented by Jung. Aphrodite appears in psychology only to be misperceived. First, she appears in erotic transference – so powerfully that Breuer flees; and Freud translates her into the inappropriate archetypal perspective of childhood and parents. But the Gods return in our diseases, as Jung said; even in that talented psychopath was the voice[49] of Aphrodite.

49 Ficino (*Commentary on Plato's Symposium* V,2) directly connects beauty with the voice.

She appears in Freud's hermeneutics of symbols understood by their genital shapes. She appears in Freud's notion of libido, whose etymon refers to *lips*, sexual desire and liquid like the sap of life. Again, instead of referring libido to the *person* of the Goddess of insemination, desire, fruit, flowers, and the visible beauty of soul, it was translated into a Promethean concept of psychic energy. How different our depth psychology would have been had we let the Goddess emerge within the psychoanalytic disease.

She appears above all in the *manifest*, not as content of it (for that remains available only to understanding), but as the manifest visible image, the displayed presentation. But again, psychological theory abandoned the manifest for the hidden – even in Jung who distinguishes psychology from aesthetics in that psychology examines its material in terms of "causal antecedents", while aesthetics regards its material as "existing in and for itself" (*CW* 15: § 135).

Approaching fantasies in terms of their causal antecedents sidesteps the impact of the image. It is deprived of its appeal, the claim of its immediate body. Something more important lurks behind – the psychodynamics by which it can be understood. The same devaluation occurs when we look at images for their symbolic contents, thereby putting in second place the form of their containment. By ignoring these formal and sensate aspects of psychic materials, we force Aphrodite to return only via her diseases – transference; sensualism, naturalism, concretism; and the flesh as sheer superficiality.

### "Going over to another order"

But what about ugliness? Surely that has been the main focus of psychotherapy. If we have neglected beauty, and the aesthetic response to the manifestation of things, we have, ever since Nietzsche, surely had a pathologizing eye, minutely scrutinizing the deformed, diseased and horrid. Perhaps, depth psychology has indeed been aesthetic but in reverse: reversing the old pairings of the good and the beautiful by "reconstructing the gibbon"[50], rather than Winckelmann's Apollo Belvedere.

Paradoxically it is through the ugly that psychology has come closest to the Neoplatonic vision. We have not been able to find Corbin's himma of the heart directly. Our theophany shows forth the Gods where they have fallen into diseases; theophany as case demonstration. The attempt of archetypal psychology to revert the diseases back to the Gods is at the same time an attempt to restore both Gods and diseases from secular ugliness. Therapy as an aesthetic undertaking requires an eye for ugliness – both delighting in and shocked by what we meet in the psyche – else we do not see the Gods at all. We see only secular human existence, case as case, demonstrating nothing beyond itself, the imagination captive in clinical anaesthesia. By attempting congruities between the imagination of the individual human soul with the imaginal patterns that myths call Gods, an archetypal therapy attempts what Freud and Jung both sought: an epistrophe of the entire civilization to its root sources, its *archai*. This reversion begins in the pathologies where the Gods are fallen, where depth psychology has always worked with its eye attentive to the ugly.

Plotinus' definition of ugly and beautiful is immediately useful for psychology. "We possess beauty when we are true to our own being; ugliness is in going over to another order" (V, 8, 13). He further tells us how we can recognize going over to another order: "Let the soul fall in with the Ugly and at once it shrinks within itself, denies the thing, turns away from it, out of tune, resenting it" (I, 6, 2). Here is the aesthetic response. When we feel cramped, resentful, out of tune, then we have gone over to another order, and have fallen (or more likely risen, since the Fall in our reversed modern world is the hybris of ego inflation) away from the soul. This means

---

50 I am referring here to the paradigmatic figures of the individuation process in Jung's *Psychology and Alchemy* (*CW 12*:§§ 164–65, 169, 175, 181) in which the "important place in the centre is reserved for the gibbon about to be reconstructed".

that soul-making can become a self-steering process through aesthetic reflexes. As important as the reflective understanding of the meaning of where we are is a sensitivity to when we go over to another order. Here, the relation to ugliness guides our self-knowledge. Ugliness is the guide because aesthetic responses occur most strongly in relation with the ugly. Plotinus says: "It must be remembered that sensations of the ugly and evil impress us more violently than those of what is agreeable... sickness makes the rougher mark... Illness... makes itself by its very incongruity" (V, i, 11)[51]. Another view of psychological illness is implied here: illness results from or is indicative of *wrong aisthesis,* and this in turn leads to an examination of the harborers of illness, not only in the invisibilities of psychodynamic conditions and fantasies of past developments, but in the aesthetic incongruities of persons and things and the visibilities of the present to the senses.

Following the signals of beauty and ugliness is an Aphroditic mode of imagining individuation. This mode maintains Psyche always in Aphrodite's temple all the while we go through the world making soul. The motto that the world is the place of soul-making, of course, comes from John Keats, and it was Keats who also said that Beauty is Truth and who said: "I am certain of nothing but the Heart's affections and the truth of Imagination" (Letter to Bailey, 22 Nov. 1817).

If we can spot these signals of imagination in the heart's affections, then we can feel when we have gone over to another order, left ourselves, and begun making illness. The aesthetic judgment is, as Kant said, independent of logic. It comes spontaneously, like a movement of the heart, even as that reaction to ugliness: "I can't stand it. Take it away. Stop. It's hideous, awful, dreadful. It makes me sick." This can be a reaction to a gesture, the sight of something, the way a person approaches, or a tone of voice. Aesthetics in everyday affairs.

---

51 Compare Plotinus on the psychological power of ugliness with the relevant passages quoted from Frances Yates *(The Art of Memory)* in my *The Myth of Analysis,* N.Y.: Harper & Row, 1978, pp. 197–98, with discussion.

The aesthetic sense perceives the form of things, apprehending the particular shape of each event, its nature disclosed by its face. These reflex reactions return psychology to that Aristotelian idea of the soul as the *form* of the body, of soul as always embodied by a form. A return to psyche as living form saves psychic phenomena from approaches defined only in terms of motion: motives, energy, dynamics. A classical idea said that Beauty arrests motion; so, too, the aesthetic response arrests those psychological theories that rely on hidden psychodynamics.

Psychology tends to forget that psyche is not only the *motion* of the body but also its *form*, so we have been forced to see the dream as running narrative (and not as image), the soul in process of growth (rather than as essence in revelation). We have lost actual form to transformation, and neglected the physiognomy of what is there, the cosmos as cosmetic face.

Aesthetic reactions are responses to this face, and moral responsibility begins in these responses of disgust, delight, abhorrence, attraction – the spontaneous judgment of the heart. "Heart, instinct, principle," said Pascal. Trust *aisthesis*, the sense of the heart; otherwise we go over to another order. I can hardly stress enough the importance of this trust, for the individual aesthetic response is also the watchdog against the Devil who slips into our lives where we least expect, dressed in the most conventional disguise. An aesthetic response is a moral response: *kalon kagathon*. Let me show you what I mean.

The novelists William Styron and George Orwell, and the social philosopher Hannah Arendt, in writing of totalitarian evil and the Nazi systematic murders in particular, have each come to the conclusion that evil is not what one expects: cruelty, moral perversion, power abuse, terror. These are its instruments or its results. But the deepest evil in the totalitarian system is precisely that which makes it work: its programmed, single-minded monotonous efficiency; bureaucratic formalism, the dulling daily service, standard, boring, letter-perfect, generalities, uniform. No thought and no responsiveness. Eichmann. Form without anima becomes formalism, conformism, formalities, formulas, office forms – forms without luster, without the presence of body. Letters without words, corporate bodies without names. All the while beauty is sequestered into the ghetto of beautiful things: museums, the ministry of culture, classical music, the dark room in the parsonage; Aphrodite imprisoned.

The "general" and the "uniform" happen in thought before they happen in the street. They happen in thought when we lose touch with our aesthetic reflexes, the heart no longer touched. The aesthetic reflex is indeed not merely disinterested aestheticism; it is our survival. So, when we are dulled, bored, an-esthetized, these emotions of bleakness are the reactions of the heart to the anaesthetic life in our civilization, events without gasping; mere banality. The ugly now is whatever we no longer notice, the simply boring, for this kills the heart. Our recourse is to Aphrodite, and our first way of discovering her is in the disease of her absence.

### The lion roars at the enraging desert

So, the question of evil, like the question of ugliness, refers primarily to the anaesthetized heart, the heart that has no reaction to what it faces, thereby turning the variegated sensuous face of the world into monotony, sameness, oneness. The desert of modernity.

Surprisingly, this desert is not heartless, because the desert is where the lion lives. There is a long-standing association of desert and lion in the same image, so that if we wish to find the responsive heart again we must go where it seems to be least present.

According to *Physiologus* (the traditional lore of animal psychology), the lion's cubs are still-born. They must be awakened into life by a roar. That is why the lion has such a roar: to awaken the young lions asleep, as they sleep in our hearts. Evidently, the thought of the heart is not simply given, a native spontaneous reaction, always ready and always there. Rather, the heart must be provoked, called forth, which is precisely Marsilio Ficino's[52] etymology of beauty; *kallos*, he says, comes from *kaleo*, provoke. "The beautiful fathers the good" (Plato, *Hipp. Maj.* 297b). Beauty must be raged, or outraged into life, for the lion's cubs are still-born, like our lazy political compliance, our meat-eating stupor before the TV set, the paralysis for which the lion's own metal, gold[53], was the paracelsian *pharmakon*. What is passive, immobile, asleep in the heart creates a desert which can only be cured by its own parenting principle that shows its awakening care by roaring. "The lion roars at the enraging desert," wrote Wallace Stevens. "Heart, instinct, principle," again Pascal.

Alongside the lion lives the desert saint. St. Paul the first hermit, St. Mary of Egypt, Euphemia, Onuphrius – each a Saint with a lion.[54] What is the relation of Saint and Lion? Is it an equation? Lion as Saint, Saint as Lion: Mark as exemplar. Does this then imply that to find the statistical saintly bit of oneself, one needs first to find the lion, the lion who lives in the heart and roars in sulphuric passion at the enraging desert?

Pelagius tells the tale of a pious anchorite who went into the desert to talk of the "wingy mysteries of divinity" with one older and wiser than he, but that old man of the desert turned away from his questions. When asked why he had refused to enter into talk, the old man said: "If he had spoken to me of the passions of the soul I could have answered him: but of the things of the spirit I am ignor-

---

52 Ficino, *loc. cit. sup.*
53 E. C. Whitmont, "Nature, Symbol, and Imaginal Reality", *Spring 1971*, p. 72, describes a psychosomatic syndrome which symbolizes with ("proves") metallic gold: "varying degrees of depression, irritability, brooding, listlessness, hopelessness... headaches, a rise of blood pressure and a disturbance of the heart function." As these patients are ill from gold, so "they are most responsive to therapeutic gold."
54 According to Jean Servier, North African Muslim Saints have been seen by pilgrims as lions and have been heard to roar. Alphonse Daudet in his *Tartarin de Tarascon* made his hero ridiculous because, in hunting a lion, he killed a domesticated one which the Brothers of Kadriya (the most popular brotherhood in North Africa) had with them when asking for alms.

ant." [The old man wanted to talk of the lion, not of wingy mysteries.] The pious anchorite hearing of this had heart-searchings, and came back to the old man and said, "What shall I do, my father, for the passions of the soul have dominion over me?" And the two talked a long while; then the anchorite was able to say: "Verily, this is love's road."[55] The more our desert the more we must rage, which rage is love.

The passions of the soul make the desert habitable. One inhabits, not a cave of rock, but the heart within the lion. The desert is not in Egypt; it is anywhere once we desert the heart. The Saints are not dead; they live in the leonine passions of the soul, in the tempting images, the sulphuric fantasies and mirages: love's road. Our way through the desert of life or any moment in life is the awakening to it as a desert, the awakening of the beast, that vigil of desire, its greedy paw, hot and sleepless as the sun, fulminating as sulphur, setting the soul on fire. Like cures like: the desert beast is our guardian in the desert of modern bureaucracy, ugly urbanism, academic trivialities, professional official soullessness, the desert of our ignoble condition.

The heart of Harvey, already dead, "fitness" replacing vitality, creates the desolation it jogs through, mufflers over the ears, blinded in the sweat of extending its life-expectancy, zombies creating the desert by running and running with nowhere to go. If beauty arrests motion, motion eradicates beauty. And the heart of Augustine fails to extend beyond the *intima mea, culpa mea*. Work it out alone, or secular sharing in group confession. Subjectivisms without rage.

We fear that rage. We dare not roar. With Auschwitz behind us and the bomb over the horizon, we let the little lions sleep in front of the television, the heart, stuffed full of its own coagulated sulphur, now become a beast in a lair readying its attack, the infarct.

Psychologically, we subdue our rage with negative euphemistic concepts: aggression, hostility, power-complex, terrorism, ambition, the problem of violence. Psychology analyzes the lion.

55 Helen Waddell, *The Desert Fathers*, London: Constable, 1936, pp. 28–29.

Perhaps Konrad Lorenz is wrong, and the counsellors wrong too, who seek to find a way beyond aggression. Is it 'aggression', or is it the lion roaring at the enraging desert? Has psychology not missed the native sulphur, neglected Mars who rides a lion, Mars, beloved of Aphrodite, demanding right. *Splendor Solis. Sol invictus:* Mithra of the heart.

Earlier we spoke of prayer. We said it was a necessary consequent to confession because it moves the heart from 'self' preoccupation into witnessing the independent power of images. In all of Plato there is only one prayer. It comes at the very end of the *Phaedrus*, that dialogue concerning beauty to which we have already referred. And it is a prayer of moral restraint. Socrates offers his prayer to Pan, and what he offers is his desire to become "fair within", "grant me beauty in the inward soul" and "as for gold, and outward things, may they not war against the spirit within me".

The curious, important fact here is that Socrates relates this beauty and restraint with Pan the Goat-God. The prayer is to the hairy-legged, animal-tailed figure unique among the major Greek divinities for his bestial shape. Socrates' prayer for beauty and limitation is to the animal-God. Could this mean that confession, too, is to the animal? Then, we go over to the other order each time we desert the animal, that saintly lion or leonine saint, who keeps us fair within and limits our reach. The heart as lion is truly king of beasts, a bestial King, and our inner beauty, our dignity, nobility, proportion, our portion of lordliness, comes as lore of character has always assumed from the animal of the heart.

### The White Sulphur and the Illusions of the Heart

If we conclude here we end in either Mithraic, martial militancy or in blind indignation, the alchemical lion eating the sun[56], consciousness devoured in its own outrage. The moral restraint that is in-

[56] *CW 12*: fig. 169.

herent to the animal, its natural piety, requires in us human beings an operation on the heart. Gods appear as animals and so the natural animal is already divine; whereas the animal that has been humanized has lost its creaturely divinity. Our lion rages and our sulphur burns. Our saint is eaten by lions. We cannot let loose our aesthetic outrage in its simple form. Alchemical psychology recognized this need for work on the lion.

Alchemical psychology considered the black and red sulphurs, and the green lion, in desperate need of subliming.[57] One well-known method cuts off the green lion's paws, depriving it of its reach into the world. Yet it stays alive as a *succus vitae* in the heart, for "green is the color of the heart and of the vitality of the heart", as we know from Corbin.[58] The color of the himma must be green like the natural driving sulphur that is also the green/red copper Goddess Venus.[59] This ardent green has to be enlightened, the sulphur chastened: a whitening of the heart.

To make white the heart is an *opus contra naturam*. We expect the heart to be red as its natural blood, green as its hopeful desire. This heart operation originates in the dilemma presented by sulphur in Part I: the imagination captive in its sulphur that both burns and co-

---

[57] Philalethes, *Secrets Reveal'd*, writes of the "Green Lion... killing all things with his Poyson" (quoted by B. J. T. Dobbs, *The Foundations of Newton's Alchemy or 'The Hunting of the Greene Lion'*, Cambridge Univ. Press, 1975, p. 68).

[58] H. Corbin, *ML*: 77-8. Further on green as colour of the soul, see Corbin, "Realisme et symbolisme des couleurs en cosmologie Shi'ite", *Eranos 41-1972*, pp. 141, 152.

[59] On Venus as green, see *CW 13*, p. 226n, where the attributes of Venus are bride, sister, air, green, green lion; and Benedictus Figulus, *A Golden Casket of Nature's Marvels*, London: Stuart & Watkins, 1963, p. 282, who warns against those "who accept Venus as sulphur", implying the illusion in assuming the *sal veneris* or green lion (= Venus) to be the whole and true nature of sulphur. The green lion and the colour green cannot be identified with any single one mineral or planet, but refer to the desirability of the world which appears as sulphur, as lion, as Venus, etc. This 'darkened' smoky green requires the illumination of the *visio smaragdina* of which Corbin writes in his *Man of Light*, an enlightening that results from an alchemical operation so that the heart's himma can reflect the sense world as images of imaginal realities.

agulates at the same instant, imagination held fused into its desire and its desire fused with its object. The himma blinded, unable to distinguish between feeling and image, image and object, object and subject, true imagining and illusion.

Alchemy often speaks of subliming to a sulphur white as snow. This is not only an operation of calming and cooling, the "Doves of Diana".[60] In fact sublimation requires going with the fire, like curing like, raising the temperature to a white heat so as to destroy all coagulations in the intensity of the desire, so that *what* one desires no longer matters, even as it matters most, mattering now sublimed, translucent, all flame.

The heart is more often whitened by its own weakening. Failures of the heart. Cowardice, nostalgia, sentimentalism, aestheticizing, doubt, vanity, withdrawal, trepidation – these emotions too arise from the heart. These are the heart's own anima states, a whitening within its own principle. Each thing must be cooked in its own blood, says alchemy. So, the red heart whitens within its own failures.

Sometimes an aesthetic reflex starts the whitening on its way: a shiver, a swoon, a need for loveliness, wanting grace more than greed, and honor as the final satisfaction – these can be indications of the lion's taming with virgin's milk. Whitening flows over the raging lion, as Aphrodite shields her warrior son, Aeneas, flowing over him, as Homer says, with her white arms and white robe (*Iliad* V, 312–15); as she herself is touched to the heart, wounded, weak, and retreats; as she withdraws her favorites from direct battle.[61]

Aphrodite whitens in other ways too: she sophisticates[62] by bringing the intelligence of wiles, deceits, persuasions, teaching the arts of intimacy and subjectivity.[63] Subjective intimacy was theologized by Augustine and became confessional; whereas the

---

60 Cf. Newton in Dobbs, *op. cit.*, pp. 171, 181.
61 Cf. Paul Friedrich, *The Meaning of Aphrodite*, Univ. of Chicago, 1978, p. 93.
62 Friedrich, *loc. cit.*, p. 123.
63 Friedrich, *loc. cit.*, for an excellent discussion of subjectivity and Sapphic poetry.

poetry of Sappho reveals Aphrodite as the archetypal person who sensitizes one to an intimacy that need not be confessional. The strident confessional subjectivity of much contemporary Sapphic poetry misses the Aphroditic touch, that sense of the sensuous beyond subjective sensation.

When the sulphur whitens within the heart, we feel at first discouraged, shrinking, in vain, nostalgic – a white longing rather than a red need – and subjectively weakened. The heart now discovers its own inhibition and, driven in on itself, it feels both its desire and its inability, passion without seizure, compulsion and impotence together, "I want" and "I can't" at once. The whitened sulphur brings to consciousness the *cor duplex*[64], the wall down the middle of our hearts which Harvey demonstrated, splitting apart that simple fantasy of untamed sulphur that the heart is whole and the heart is one.

The wall down the middle of our hearts necessitates the complex circulation of the heart's contents – its imagination and its responses – to the periphery of our beings, making us all heart, heart all through us, as Avicenna's physiology said a thousand years ago.[65] This bifurcated and dislocated heart results from these operations of whitening, so that the heart may no longer be only the literal organ and the literal outrage of the royal monistic lion. Now its thought moves widely around, always in motion as reactions and aesthetic responses. There is a circulation of the light in the circulation of the blood[66], thinking in the skin and in the feet, in the throat and temple

---

64 The *dipsychos*, or double-hearted, is a rare term of moral opprobrium in the Bible meaning simulation, even lying. (Cf. *Le Cœur* – Etudes Carmélitaines, Bruges: Desclée de Brouwer, 1950, p. 67.) By upholding the simplicity of the heart, the Church tradition makes either simplistic or abysmal the complexity of the heart's capacity for deception which this section of my paper is trying to differentiate.

65 "The heart to anatomy is a circumscribed organ; to Avicenna it is part of a force occupying the whole body." O. C. Gruner, *The Canon of Medicine of Avicenna*, London: Luzac, 1930, p. 12. The "whole body" can be understood as the "volume" *(jism)*, i.e., the fullest amplification of the heart. (Cf. *SB*: 180f.)

66 By light in the blood I refer to the circulation of consciousness throughout all senses which has its parallels in the circulation of the light (*CW 13*: 27–82), and

pulses; the "least pulses of my body shook," as Dante said on seeing Beatrice. This heart acts not as central king or pump, but as the circulation itself, sensitive to many things in many places, its red passion whitened to compassion.

Besides the weakening, sophistication and circulation, the heart whitens in yet another way: through its own illusions. Any explication of the heart's thought must also account for the heart's illusions: that we fall wrongly in love, delight in bad tastes, follow a false flag, father a betrayer, stand loyal to hollow codes, braggadocio, kitsch. These too are signs of the lion. What heart does not go "over to the other side", deluded by its leonine conviction, especially that most heartfelt delusion of its faith in its feelings as its own truth.

The illusions of the heart must be grounded in the same place as its truths. Those condemnations of the heart which reach back to the dawn of philosophy have always blamed it for opinion, subjectivism, illusion, and clinging to the world of untrustworthy sense. Yes, why not? Imagination begins in a heart aware that there is both true and false imagining, and that they are not contradictories, but rather co-relatives, even co-terminous. We cannot have the true without the false. We recognize true imagining by means of a subtle sense of illusions, a sensitivity to going off wrong. The sophistication of the heart is its double-beat, an echoing syncopation; or its

---

even more in the "rose-coloured blood" in alchemy (383–91, 433), where the blood red lightens to rose red indicating, among other things, the heightened sensitization of the five senses: "Praise me in my five senses, which are indicated by this rose" (p. 388). Of course, the flower, rose, in antiquity belonged to Isis, Aphrodite, Venus, Dionysus, the Muses and Graces (Barbara Seward, *The Symbolic Rose*, N.Y.: Columbia Univ. Press, 1960, pp. 1–17). Gertrude Stein expressed the circulation of the rose in her paradigmatic sentence, "a rose is a rose is a rose". Again, we must not miss that it is particularly the most sulphuric and 'animalistic' sense of smell that correlates with the rose-coloured blood, for the text which Jung quotes (p. 388) goes on to say: "through the sense of smell he [Christ] has always a certain loving affection directed towards man." I have expanded on smell in both *The Dream and the Underworld*, N.Y.: Harper, pp. 185–88, and in my "Image-Sense", *Spring 1979*, pp. 139–43.

*The Thought of the Heart*

interior wall, a two-sided mirror by means of which reflective speculations may be taken to heart and imagined further. Only this interior reverberation allows the heart to witness the images in its feelings rather than to be identified with its feelings in that subjectivism which is the ground of all false imagining. Remember, himma presents the images of the heart as essentially, though intimately[67], real; yet the reality of its persons is independent of my person.

Thus we can affirm the heart's illusions as necessary for the sophistication of its imaginings. It will be aware that its realities are not real and its irrealities are real, that its feelings are its truth and yet these feelings are fantasies of its desire and auras of its images, that as it loves it lies to further invent its love, and that the sensate sulphuric world with which it burns is so compelling because of our heart-hunger for forms, for beauty, which that sensate world embodies. The heart would be touched, asks that the world touch it with tastes and sounds and smells; *aisthesis*; touched by the image.

\*

I have tried in this talk to restore the animal sense to imagining by remembering the lion in the heart before Harvey, before Augustine. This heart awakens in the aesthetic response. It is an animal awareness to the face of things. I have also tried to connect this animal awareness with the himma, suggesting that it is by means of the lion in the heart that we perceive and respond imaginally. As Corbin has written: "... certain of our traditions... mention that animals *see* things which, among human beings, can be seen only by visionary

---

67 The "intimate taste" *(dhawq)* of imagining (*CI*: 221–22) depends on the himma. Combining this notion of intimacy with that of Wm. James (I, note 8), it seems we can become intimate with an image or a thing in a sensuous way only when we have abandoned the rational account of it. Intimacy, whether in Sappho, Corbin or James, depends on the experience of the particular as such; this gives us a new way of understanding Aristotle's phrase "It would seem that experience of particular things is a sort of courage" (*N. Eth.* 3.11.1116b).

mystics. It is possible that this animal vision takes place in the absolute *mundus archetypus*..." (*SB*: 146).

This thought of the heart returns us to an animal thought, intimacy released from confession into immediacy, the courage of immediate intimacy, and not merely with ourselves, but with the particular faces of the sensate world with which our heart is in rapport like a watching animal in its lair, a guardian angel of survival who knows each time we go over to the other side.

For us each to become "fair within" we need to let this lion bring its decorum into our behaviour. In the blood of the animal is an archetypal mind, a mindfulness, a carefulness in regard to each particular thing. And this minding of events arises in the reactions of the heart, neither as mere personal feelings, nor as a mechanical mindlessness of the Harveyein heart that does not consider, does not conceive. With the lion lives the saint, by which I mean that sense of restraint incumbent upon being perceived by the animated world in which is the presence of Aphrodite with whom the saint always contends. To be is to be perceived[68] – by her, by them. It is not merely *our* aesthetic reactions, but *theirs* to us. Not the subject an observer as in a scientific universe, all things turning around one subject, but the subject, ourselves, subjected to the gaze of things, ourselves a display. To the ensouled world we too are objects of *aisthesis*, aesthetically breathed in by the *anima mundi*, perceived by her, perhaps, even, aesthetically breathed out as images by an ardent himma in the heart of each thing.

---

[68] "*Esse* is *percipi*" from George Berkeley was the motto of my Eranos lecture in 1976, where its psychological significance is discussed further (*Eranos 45–1976*, p. 221).